IMAGES
of America

UNION CITY

IMAGES

of America

UNION CITY

Timothy Swenson

ARCADIA
PUBLISHING

Published by Arcadia Publishing
Charleston SC, Chicago IL, Portsmouth NH, San Francisco CA

Library of Congress Catalog Card Number: 2007939183

For all general information contact Arcadia Publishing at:
Telephone 843-853-2070
Fax 843-853-0044
E-mail sales@arcadiapublishing.com
For customer service and orders:
Toll-Free 1-888-313-2665

Visit us on the Internet at www.arcadiapublishing.com

To my family: my wife, Catherine; daughters Caitlan, Ashlyn, and Megan; my father, Charles; my mother, Linda; and my brother, Tony

CONTENTS

ACKNOWLEDGMENTS

This book is based on the work of those who have come before me. The Dr. Robert B. Fisher Collection is the single best collection of photographs in Washington Township. Combining that with other photograph collections, the Museum of Local History has the finest overall collection of photographs in Washington Township. I am also indebted to those who have researched and written on local history. These authors are listed in the bibliography. Without those who documented history in both written and photographic form, we would have no history.

I would like to thank the Museum of Local History for making the majority of the photographs in this book available. I would also like to thank those individuals and organizations that also donated photographs and/or provided research assistance, including Gil Prevette, Alice Robie, Lupe St. Denis, Al Rose, Karl Vincent, Norman Silveira, Carol Dutra-Vernaci, Ann Riojas, Heidi Kitayama, Dick Oliver, police chief Stewart, Hillview Baptist Church, Our Lady of the Rosary Church, and the Union City Historical Museum.

All photographs are part of the Museum of Local History collections, including the Dr. Robert B. Fisher Collection, unless otherwise noted.

INTRODUCTION

Union City sits on the east side of the San Francisco Bay Area, bordered by Hayward on the north, Fremont on the south, on the east by the hills, and on the west by the bay. Union City is suburbia with a mix of structures for housing, shopping, and industrial uses.

There was another Union City before there was the current Union City. In 1851, John Horner built a landing on Alameda Creek at a large bend. He laid out a town and called it Union City, named after the steamship *Union* he owned. At about the same time, Henry C. Smith created the town of New Haven less than a mile west of Horner's Union City. The two towns would eventually merge and be known as Alvarado, named after Juan B. Alvarado, a Mexican governor of California.

In the early 1850s, Alvarado was the commerce center of Alameda County. Goods from the farms in the area were shipped to the rapidly growing town of San Francisco. Hard goods were shipped from San Francisco to Alvarado to be sold through local mercantile stores. In 1870, the first successful sugar beet factory was started by E. H. Dyer and located just at the edge of Alvarado.

With the coming of the transcontinental railroad in 1869, the town of Decoto was established on land owned by the Decoto brothers. Decoto was mostly known for farming; just after the start of the 20th century, canneries would come to Decoto to package and ship local produce. In 1937, the Pacific States Steel opened south of Decoto and would become the largest employer in the town for 40 years.

After Decoto was almost incorporated by Hayward, local leaders decided to move and merge the towns of Decoto and Alvarado. On January 13, 1959, an election was held on incorporation, which passed. On Monday, January 26, 1959, at 2:00 p.m., Union City became official. The city council was sworn in with Tom Kitayama, John Ratekin, Joseph Seaone, Oscar Dowe, and Joseph Lewis. The first action the city council took was to appoint Tom Kitayama as mayor.

Union City would start out as a small town with a population of 6,000 and lots of farm fields. In 50 years, the population would climb to more than 70,000 and the fields would be turned into homes, shopping centers, schools, and industrial parks.

In 2009, Union City turns 50 years old. A citizen-run nonprofit, the 50th Anniversary Celebration Committee, with help from local businesses and the City of Union City, is planning a number of events scheduled throughout the year, including galas at both the start and end of the year.

One

ALVARADO

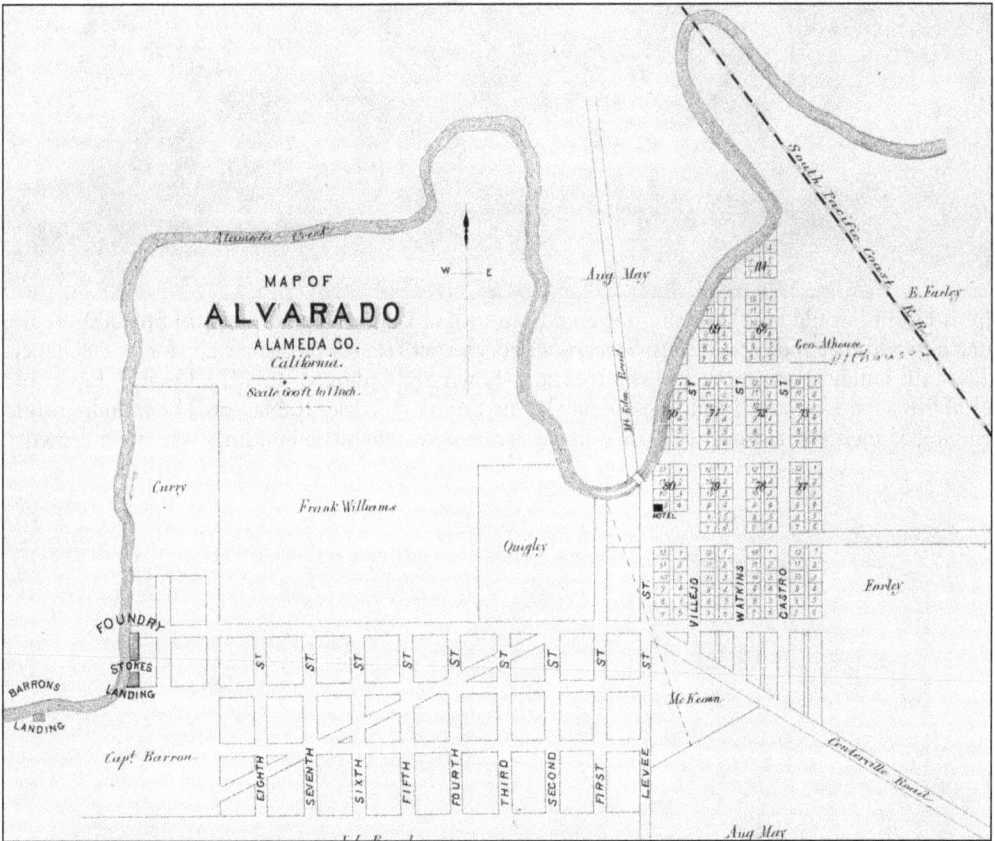

In 1878, Thompson and West published an atlas of Alameda County containing an early map of Alvarado. The left side (west) shows the two landings owned by Richard Barron and J. J. Stokes. Property tracks and their owners are detailed on the map, which shows land owned by well-known pioneers like John Quigley, J. L. Beard, and August May. This map is more of a plan for Alvarado, as older maps do not show Watkins Street extending to the south of Smith Street and Castro Street was not built.

John Horner would build a steam-powered flour mill at Union City at a cost of $85,000. At the first agricultural exposition held in San Francisco, Horner's flour won a silver cup for its excellence. The mill building was moved to the location shown and enlarged. In 1870, George Tay would establish a foundry in the buildings under the direction of Charles R. Nauert. The foundry would employ 35 men and close in 1920. It is unknown exactly when the buildings were demolished.

In 1851, John Horner built a landing at a bend in Alameda Creek and constructed a number of warehouses. Horner would plot out a town and called it Union City, named after the steamship *Union* that he bought to ship goods to San Francisco. J. J. Stokes would own the landing in 1878. Benson, then Richard Barron, would own a landing next to Horner's landing. Barron would use the name Union City Landing well into the late 1800s. This photograph was taken in 1903.

For many years, Alameda Creek was used for shipping to move produce to market in San Francisco. This photograph shows a small boat motoring west with the Union City Landing warehouse buildings in the background. Eventually Alameda Creek would silt up and make navigation impossible.

Andrew Henderson Broder was the first sheriff of Alameda County when it was formed in 1853. In the first election in Alameda County, held April 24, 1853, Andrew Broder was elected as sheriff and tax collector. He would be elected to both of these posts for the next three years. Since there was no jail, early criminals were locked up in the Brooklyn Hotel. One of the early crimes Sheriff Broder investigated was the theft of state and county funds from the office of county treasurer J. S. Marsten. This wedding photograph from 1854 shows Broder with Sara Ann Smith, the sister of Henry C. Smith.

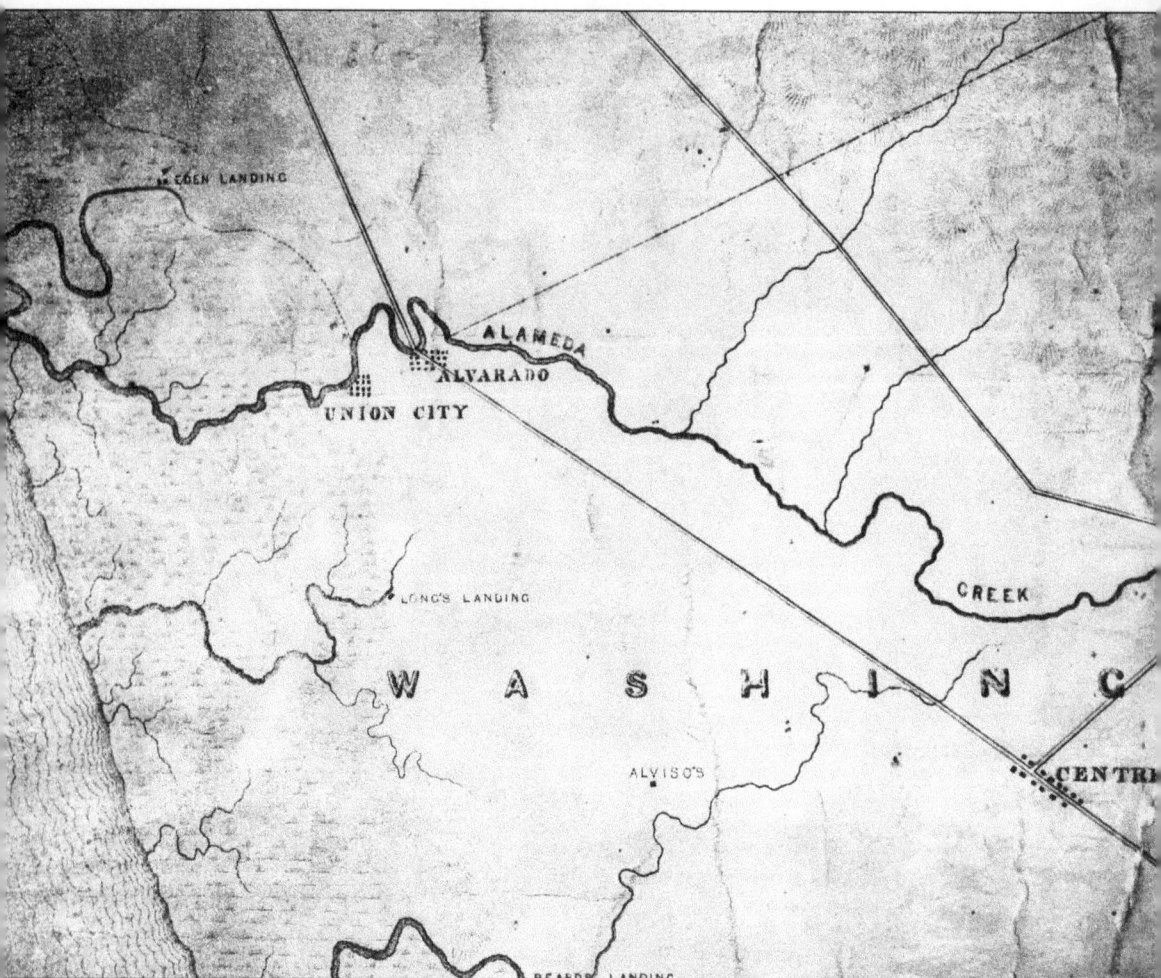

John Horner founded Union City at a bend in Alameda Creek that was being used by Mission San Jose for shipping. Just to the east, Henry Smith founded New Haven close to another bend in Alameda Creek called the Devil's Elbow. Eventually New Haven would become Alvarado. At first, Union City would show up on the maps as a separate town, like on this late-1850s map. By the next century, most residents would refer to both towns as Alvarado. This map also shows the road coming from Hayward through Alvarado and then to Centerville.

No. 12   Union City, *Aug* 20 1870

Received in Barron's Union City Warehouse,

the following Mdse. for account of *S. P. Harvey*

on Storage, at _____ per ton in Gold Coin, per season ending June 1st. 187_

MARKS.	NUMBERS.	DESCRIPTION.
	499 525	Sacks Barley
	150	Sacks Wheat
		James Barron

John Horner would sell his warehouse and landing at Union City. Richard Barron would purchase the landing and later sell it to his brother James about the time that Richard would purchase Mount Eden landing, a few miles north. This receipt is for sacks of wheat and barley stored at the warehouse on August 20, 1870, for S. P. Harvey. Even in 1870, Union City was still distinct from Alvarado.

Standing on the west side of Levee Street was an old brick building that was a saloon for many years. This photograph shows a number of patrons standing in front of the saloon. The windows advertise "wine and liquors" and 5¢ beer.

This photograph shows many of the early founders of Alvarado. The small numbers were added by William Jung and show (10) John Lyman Beard, (17) ? Osgood, (25) Howard Overacker, (28) William Liston, (29) Joseph McKeown, (37) F. B. Granger, and (40) George Patterson. (Courtesy Alice Robie.)

After establishing New Haven, later Alvarado, Henry C. Smith built a home at the end of Vallejo Street. Constructed in 1852, it existed in 1953 but does not exist today.

Capt. William Liston came to Union City in 1851 to work for Henry C. Smith. He was a member of the Alvarado Home Guard, which was formed in August 1863. His home, built about 1860, survived at least into the 1970s when this photograph was taken.

William Liston helped form the Crusade Lodge of the Odd Fellows and the Pioneer Society in 1876. This is a side view of his house on what appears to be Vallejo Street.

This is another view of the Liston house from the 1970s. The 1870s census shows that William, his wife, Catherine, and their children Margaret and James living in Alvarado.

In the early days of Alvarado, the nearest Catholic church was located at Mission San Jose. In 1862, St. Anne's Catholic Church was built to provide a closer house of worship. For many years, the church would be a mission church, meaning that the priest was from another church and would come in on Sunday for service. At the time, most of the parishioners were from Portugal, so the services were given in Portuguese.

The largest mechanical firm in Alvarado was the carriage works of Joseph McKeown. The building was lost to fire in 1890.

Pictured is Joseph McKeown, the owner of the carriage works in Alvarado. He served in the Alvarado Guard as second lieutenant. He also petitioned the state for the creation of Alameda County. He was appointed to the board of education in 1880. He would serve as treasurer of Odd Fellows Crusader Lodge in 1883.

Pictured is James McKeown, brother to Joseph McKeown. Both men were originally from Ireland.

Annie McKeown, the wife of James McKeown, is pictured here. Born in 1851, Annie passed away in 1929 at the age of 78.

In 1886, James Hawley and his wife, Betty (sitting in front on the porch), celebrated their 60th wedding anniversary with a large gathering of family. James would pass away a year later, but Betty would live until 1911. The Hawley family had a number of daughters who married into other pioneer families, such as the Whipples and Ingalls.

A close-up of the Hawley family shows James, his wife, Betty, and daughters Emily Hawley Ingalls, Loretta Volmer, and Charlotte Heyers.

Farley B. Granger came to Alvarado in 1861 and purchased land for farming. He would sell part of his land to the Dyers for the sugar beet factory. He built the Riverside Hotel near the Alvarado rail depot. Granger would purchase the old Union City Landing wharves, where he developed an artesian water company. This would be sold to the Oakland Water Company.

Pictured is the exterior view of the Riverside Hotel, facing west on what is now New Haven Street, close to the Alvarado train station.

Another view of the Riverside Hotel is shown here. The hotel would survive for many years, but it would burn down because of a fire rumored to be started by vagrants living in the building.

GRAND OPENING BALL

RIVERSIDE HOTEL

ALVARADO

Tuesday Evening, December 24th, 1878

MUSIC BY BLUM'S BAND.

Tickets, admitting Gentleman and Ladies, including Supper,   -   -   -   -   - $2.50

The Riverside Hotel, close to the Alvarado Train Station, was opened in 1878. The Grand Opening Ball was held on December 24, 1878, as shown on this ticket. The cost of the dinner for a couple was $2.50. The grand opening was the highlight of the year.

In the late 1800s, a number of different salt works would be built in the Alvarado area. Saltwater marsh would be converted to salt ponds for the drying of saltwater to form salt crystals. When harvested, the salt was piled up, as can be seen here. This photograph is of the Crystal Salt Works, owned by John Plummer and situated south of Alvarado.

JOHN W. SINCLAIR,
OCCIDENTAL SALT WORK
Alvarado, Cal.

A salt works, one of several, that was started near Alvarado was the Occidental Salt Works. By 1936, all of the salt works in southern Alameda County would be consolidated into Leslie Salt with its factory in Newark.

Another salt works was Turk Island Salt Works, located near a small hillock known as Turk Island. With large sections of the bay marsh converted to shallow ponds rich in brine shrimp, flocks of birds would use the ponds during their annual migration. Duck hunting was a popular pastime. Two duck hunting clubs would be founded just after 1900 and would continue until the late 1990s, when encroaching homes would shut them down.

The annual floods covered a large area of Alvarado, including the Turk Island Salt Works. This picture of the 1883 flood shows a farmhouse surrounded by shallow water.

The International Order of Odd Fellows (IOOF) was founded in Alvarado on November 26, 1859. Well-known charter members were Charles Eigenbrodt, E. H. Dyer, James Hawley, and William Liston. In 1864, the Odd Fellows Hall was built at the corner of Smith and Vallejo Streets by the Odd Fellows Hall Association. The building was two stories, 40 feet wide, and 65 feet long. The Odd Fellows would use the upstairs of the building for their meetings. The downstairs would be used for dancing and, later, movies. The building would be demolished in 1967.

This picture shows another view of the Odd Fellows Hall, whose initials are shown on the building. The hall would also be used by other fraternal organizations, such as the Native Sons of the Golden West and the Ancient Order of United Workmen.

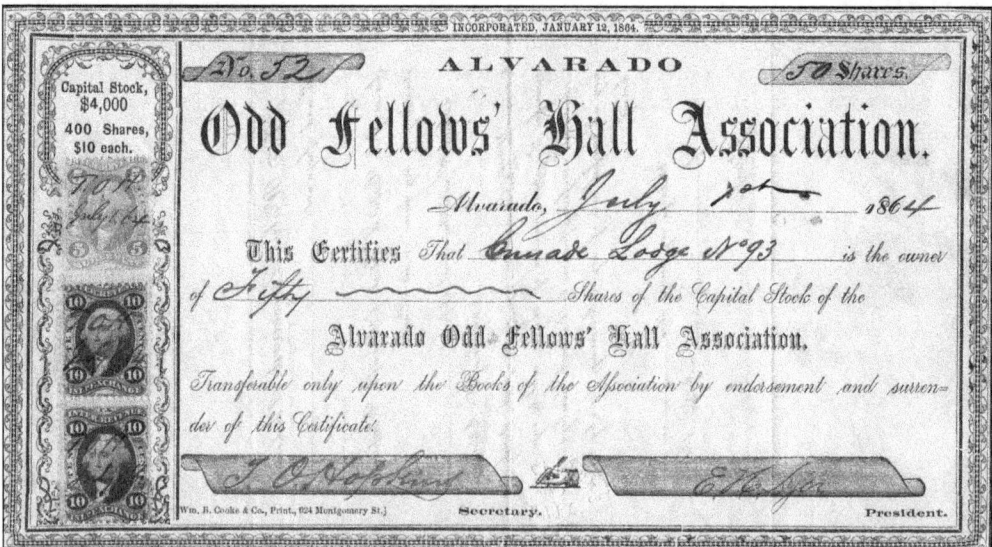

To build the Odd Fellows Hall, the Crusader Lodge No. 93 organized the Odd Fellows Hall Association and sold shares to raise money. The lodge sold 400 shares at $10 each for a total of $4,000. This stock certificate shows that the lodge itself purchased 50 shares in July 1864. At the time, the secretary was E. H. Dyer. (Courtesy Al Rose.)

The original flag used by the Alvarado Home Guard in 1864 was preserved and displayed in the Odd Fellows Hall.

Chinese were early immigrants to Alvarado. They would be the primary laborers for the sugar beet factory and local farmworkers. Eventually a Chinatown would develop in Alvarado. Running along the north side of Smith Street for about 75 yards, starting about where Fredi Street is now, were a number of Chinese businesses including a laundry. Oral histories state that both gambling and prostitution were also available in Chinatown. Sometime in the late 1920s, the local citizens emptied Chinatown, sending the residents to Oakland and setting the buildings on fire.

The Hong Lee Alvarado Laundry along Smith Street was also part of Chinatown.

On the corner of Watkins and Smith Streets was the Loyola house, used for a number of years as a preschool and day care by Isabel Loyola. It was torn down in 1999.

Pictured is a view of Levee Street (Union City Boulevard) from Horner Street in the foreground to Smith Street in the background.

Levee Street, now Union City Boulevard, was the main north-to-south street in Alvarado. This photograph shows Levee Street, looking north, from present-day Horner Street. Hotel Chantecler and the Ralph and Harvey General Store are seen on the right. Farther down is the Alvarado Hotel.

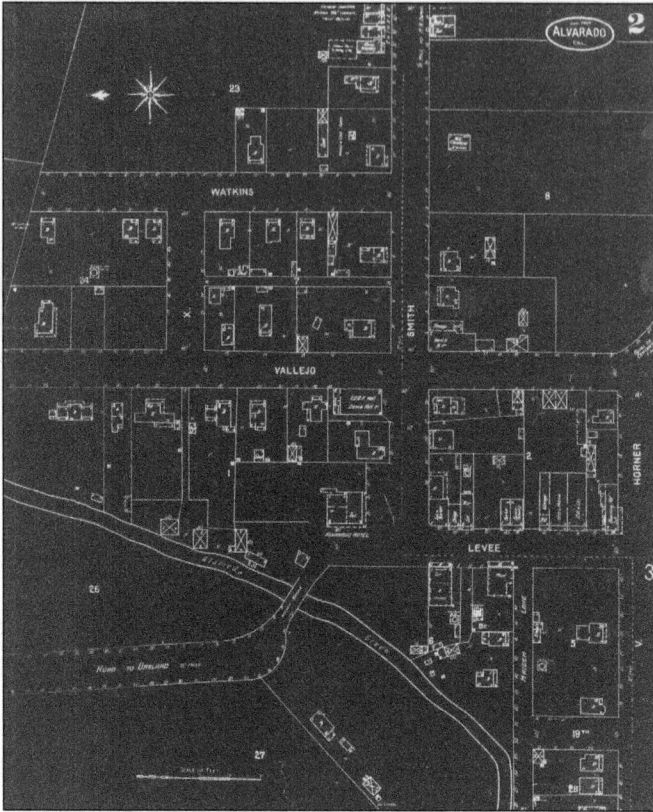

This Sanborn map shows Alvarado in 1901. The layout of the streets is pretty much the same as it is now. The map shows Smith, Vallejo, Watkins, and Levee Streets. At the bottom of the map is Alameda Creek's location as it was for many years. Later it would be moved more to the north so flooding would not affect Alvarado as much. Sanborn maps were created by the Sanborn Company for fire insurance purposes.

This shows a more expansive view down Levee Street in 1912. On the right is the Hotel Chantecler, and next to it is the Ralph and Scribner store. Farther down the street is the Alvarado Hotel.

The first bridge over Alameda Creek was built in 1853 by the Horner brothers, John and William. Known as the Smith Street Bridge, it was built near the present intersection of Smith Street and Dyer Road. It cost the Horner Brothers $1,100 to build. It would later be replaced with a concrete bridge. As Alameda Creek was routed through a flood-control channel just south of Union City, the bridge was no longer needed so a grade-level crossing of the older creek was put in.

Just east of downtown Alvarado, Smith Street crossed Alameda Creek. This picture from March 1928 shows the height of the river flowing under the bridge.

Constructed in the early 1900s, this building held a saloon and a barbershop run by Tony Mello. Although shown as rundown in this photograph, the building was renovated and is being used today for a number of businesses.

In 1862, the Alvarado Hotel was built at the corner of Smith Street and Levee Street (now Union City Boulevard). It was originally a boardinghouse for foundry workers and boat passengers. In the late 1800s, the hotel was operated by the Hennigsen brothers. The hotel was remodeled in 1947 by Fernandes Parades at a cost of $25,000, giving it a more Spanish-style look. The roof was flattened and the wraparound porch removed. The building still stands today.

This photograph shows an early view down Levee Street with a couple of residents, including one with his dogs. The building on the far right is where the Hotel Chantecler was later built.

This is the home of James McKeown, a brother to Joseph McKeown. James was a director of the Alvarado Presbyterian Church when the church was built in 1902.

January 1916 would bring another flood to Alvarado. This photograph shows the flooding was not deep, just extensive.

The close proximity of Alameda Creek to Alvarado was the cause of many floods. It was the annual floods that caused the county seat to be moved from Alvarado to San Leandro. The floods would stop residents from reaching the courthouse. This picture shows Alvarado-Niles Road flooding in the 1930s. The house on the right belonged to the Dyer family.

The sugar beet pulp, left over from the sugar extraction process, was fed to cattle. In this photograph, the cattle barns can be seen with the factory in the background. (Courtesy Alice Robie.)

Smith Street is one of the major streets in Alvarado. This photograph from 1890 shows the Odd Fellows Hall on the left and the Harvey, later Dinsmore, store (a general store) on the right. Notice the horse hitching post next to the brick building.

Built in 1878, this two-story, four-room schoolhouse for Alvarado was the fourth structure used in Alvarado as a school. Charlotte Jung was a teacher there. The school would continue until a new one was built in 1924.

A very early photograph shows the students of Alvarado Grammar School.

Pictured is the Alvarado Grammar School class from around 1907 to 1910 with Albert Norris, the school superintendent. (Courtesy Alice Robie.)

The Alvarado Grammar School was built in 1878 on the property of the current Alvarado Elementary School. It was a two-story, four-room building that would be used until 1924, when a newer school was built. The 1924 elementary school was replaced by the modern one in the 1950s.

The Bank of Alvarado was founded in 1902 by I. V. Ralph. In 1908, August May Jr. would take over as president of the bank. In 1910, the name would be changed to the Bank of Alameda County and a branch would be opened in Irvington. In 1916, the Bank of Niles was bought and became a branch of the Bank of Alameda County.

The Alvarado Presbyterian Church is shown here. The 1862 church building is on the left-hand side. In 1902, a new larger church was built and the older church was demolished. Eventually Brooklyn Street would be put in right where the older church stood.

The Alvarado Presbyterian Church found they needed a larger church for their congregation. As soon as the new church was built in 1902, the older church was demolished. This photograph catches the very instant the steeple was toppled. The newer church would later be sold to a different denomination. Where the older church stood, Brooklyn Street was built.

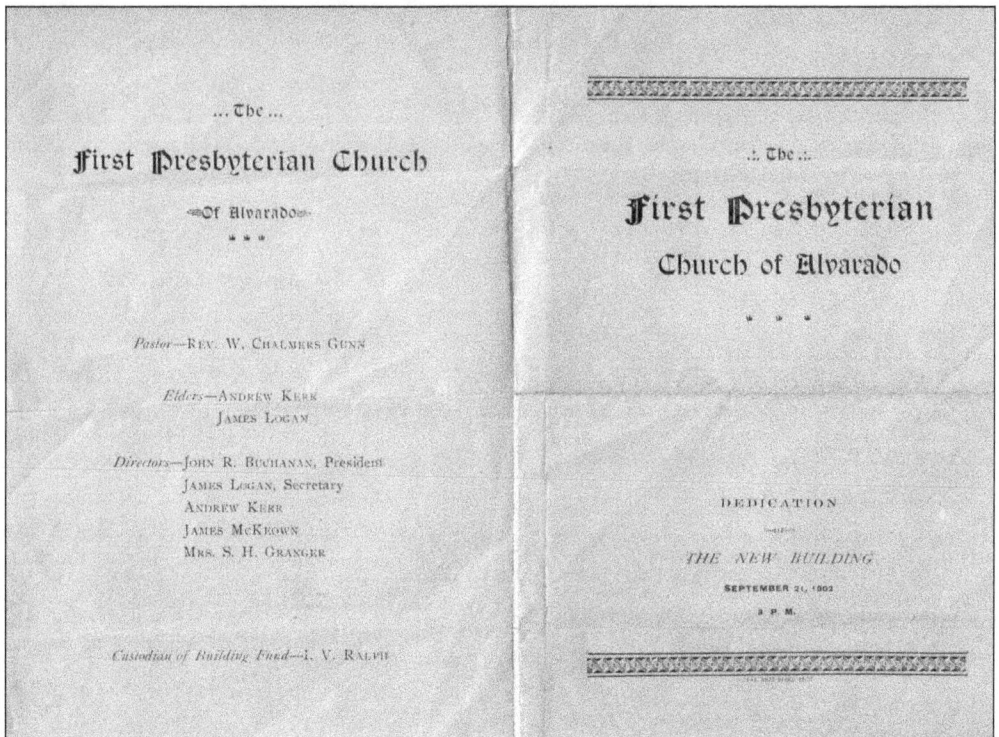

... The ...

First Presbyterian Church

—Of Alvarado—

* * *

Pastor—REV. W. CHALMERS GUNN

Elders—ANDREW KERR
JAMES LOGAN

Directors—JOHN R. BUCHANAN, President
JAMES LOGAN, Secretary
ANDREW KERR
JAMES McKEOWN
MRS. S. H. GRANGER

Custodian of Building Fund—I. V. RALPH

.:. The .:.

First Presbyterian

Church of Alvarado

* * *

DEDICATION

THE NEW BUILDING

SEPTEMBER 21, 1902

3 P. M.

The second church for the Alvarado Presbyterian Church was dedicated on September 21, 1902. This cover of the dedication program shows the names of the pastor, elders, and directors for the church. (Courtesy Alice Robie.)

Standing behind the Loyola house, these distinguished gentlemen seem to be dressed up for some event. (Courtesy Lupe St. Denis.)

This receipt from the South Pacific Coast Railroad shows William Liston paid for the shipment of three cases of paint from San Francisco to Alvarado in August 1878. (Courtesy Al Rose.)

In 1878, the South Pacific Coast Railroad was built through Alvarado. The railroad built the Alvarado train station to handle the local shipping needs. The train station, also built in 1878, was of a type typical for the South Pacific Coast Railroad, with other train stations along the line having similar details. In 1976, the building was torn down. This photograph is from 1972.

Ebenezer Herrick (E. H.) Dyer came to Alvarado in 1858. In 1859, he was elected county surveyor and in 1861 appointed U.S. deputy surveyor, a position he served in for 10 years. He founded the Alvarado sugar beet factory in 1879 as the Standard Sugar Manufacturing Company. With his brother Ephraim, his sons and in-laws, and the Ingalls, Ebenezer was able to have one of the longest-running businesses in Union City.

In 1878, the South Pacific Coast Railroad would build a rail line from Santa Cruz through San Jose and then to Oakland. The main rail stop for the South Pacific Coast Railroad in Union City was in Alvarado. The station was built in 1878. It was used for many years for both passenger and freight traffic. Eventually the railroad no longer needed a stop in Alvarado, and the station was closed. In 1976, the station, at the end of New Haven Street next to the present railroad tracks, was torn down.

This photograph only had the name Dyer on the back. Compared to an earlier etching, it appears to be E. H. Dyer.

In 1887, a boiler explosion devastated the sugar beet factory and killed one worker. The factory was closed, but the next year, the Dyer brothers and sons reorganized and formed a new company, the Pacific Coast Sugar Company, and rebuilt the factory.

Another view of the 1887 boiler explosion at the sugar factory is pictured here.

E. H. Dyer built a home near the sugar beet factory. He put his office in the small top story of the home. From there, he would design a number of other sugar beet factories that his company would build worldwide.

The Alvarado sugar beet factory was incorporated under a number of different names, the first being California Beet Sugar Manufacturing Company. It was later named Standard Sugar Refining Company and Alameda Sugar Company. It was bought in 1927 by the Holly Sugar Corporation.

The Alvarado sugar beet factory was named Alameda Sugar Company from 1889 to 1927. During those years, it processed about 1.6 million tons of beets, with the plant being idle in 1914. In 1889, the processing capacity was 300 tons, and by 1924, it was at 900 tons.

As time went by, the sugar beet factory would take on many corporate names. In 1889, it was named the Alameda Sugar Company and would remain that way until the factory was bought by Holly Sugar in 1927. (Courtesy Lupe St. Denis.)

When the sugar beet factory was built, the only way to ship goods from there was via Alameda Creek. When the South Pacific Coast Railroad was put through Alvarado, a spur would be created for the sugar factory, allowing them to receive beets and send the finished sugar via rail. Eventually Alameda Creek would silt over so that shipping via boat was not feasible.

In the late 1920s, after Holly Sugar purchased the Alvarado sugar beet factory, the older wooden factory was torn down and a new safer metal factory was constructed. The buildings were torn down carefully as the large equipment inside was going to be used in the new factory. (Courtesy Norman Silveira.)

Here is an inside view of the boilers used by the Alvarado sugar beet factory to boil down the beet juice after it was pressed from the beets. (Courtesy Norman Silveira.)

The signature structure on the Alvarado sugar beet factory was the huge smokestack. This picture shows the early construction of the smokestack. (Courtesy Norman Silveira.)

This aerial photograph of the sugar beet factory, taken around 1950, shows the last version of the factory, which was built in the early 1930s. The well-known smokestack stands out in the middle of the photograph. The trees running from left to right show the path of Alameda Creek. After the creek was no longer usable for shipping, a rail siding was put in on the Southern Pacific Railroad to service the factory.

This view of the Alvarado sugar beet factory shows the newer factory being built and the signature smokestack.

Silvester P. Harvey joined in the mercantile business with John Ralph. This photograph is of his home. Silvester was one of the early founders of the Alvarado Presbyterian Church.

John Ralph owned a store with Harvey on what is now Union City Boulevard. Later Scribner would purchase the Harvey half of the business. This picture shows the interior of the store with Ralph (right) and Scribner. (Courtesy Lupe St. Denis.)

This picture shows another view of the interior of the Ralph and Scribner store showing Scribner (center) and Ralph (left). (Courtesy Lupe St. Denis.)

This is an outside view of the Ralph and Scribner store on Levee Street.

The Ralphs and Scribners lived just a couple of homes away from each other. This picture is of John Ralph sitting in the chair and Scribner resting his head on his hand. Both of their homes still stand today on Vallejo Street. (Courtesy Lupe St. Denis.)

This home on Vallejo Street was owned by the Joyce and Scribner families. Built around 1870, it was also owned by I. V. Ralph.

Another view of the Joyce/Scribner home is shown here just a few doors down from the home of John Ralph, the business partner of Scribner.

This photograph shows the first wife of John Ralph. When she passed away, John would remarry and the second Mrs. Ralph would live in the Ralph house on Vallejo Street for many years. (Courtesy Lupe St. Denis.)

Taken during an outing, some Alvarado residents are pictured here. From left to right are (first row) two unidentified women, Mrs. Ralph, Jennie Decoto May, and two unidentified women; (second row) Mr. Scribner, Mrs. Scribner, August May Jr., and an unidentified woman. (Courtesy Lupe St. Denis.)

John Ralph was the fire chief when the Alvarado Fire District was formed in 1905. In 1940, this district was dissolved and a new one was formed. In the middle of this photograph is John Ralph, and at right is his second wife. The other lady is unidentified. (Courtesy Lupe St. Denis.)

This photograph shows, from left to right, Gloria Naber, Russel Norris, and Russel's sister Alma Norris. The Norris family was a leading Alvarado family in the early 20th century. (Courtesy Alice Robie.)

Another photograph shows the Alvarado train station, with Alma Norris on the left and possibly Gloria Naber standing. (Courtesy Alice Robie.)

As with most small towns, one of the more interesting ways to spend time in Alvarado was to head out to the train depot to see who was coming and going. In this photograph is Gus Rutherford, the Alvarado stationmaster. The woman standing up is Alma Norris, and her friend Gloria Naber is seated. (Courtesy Alice Robie.)

This is a 1940s picture of Alma Norris after she married William Russell Robie. (Courtesy Alice Robie.)

This photograph shows Albert Norris Sr. with his granddaughter Marjorie standing on Smith Street with the Dinsmore store in the background. Albert was the Alvarado postmaster from 1915 to 1934. (Courtesy Alice Robie.)

Pictured is William Russell Robie at the Alvarado sugar beet factory. (Courtesy Alice Robie.)

William Jung was in the meat business with Frederich Wiegman for a short time. William and his family lived in a house on Vallejo Street between the Scribner and Ralph homes. The home was located on what is now an empty lot next to the Scribner home. (Courtesy Alice Robie.)

Born in 1859, Christina Penke Jung celebrates her 100th birthday with her family. Standing on the left with grey hair and glasses is her daughter Charlotte Jung, a longtime teacher at Alvarado Elementary School. (Courtesy Alice Robie.)

STATE OF CALIFORNIA

No. 12810

COUNTY OF ALAMEDA

POLL TAX RECEIPT TWO DOLLARS

May 12 1905

Received of _Farley Granger_

TWO DOLLARS, being his Poll Tax for the year 1905

HENRY P. DALTON, Assessor,

County Treasurer

G. W. Bacon

County Auditor.

By _J. D. Witherly_

DEPUTY ASSESSOR.

A poll tax is a "head" tax paid by each person seeking to vote. In some communities, it was an important source of income even into the early 20th century. The receipt shows that Farley Granger Jr. paid his annual $2 poll tax for 1905. Farley B. Granger is the son of Farley Granger Sr., who came to Alvarado in 1861 and became a farmer.

SPECIAL ELECTION, Tuesday, August 13, 1935

Your polling place is

Riverside Hotel

DO NOT DESTROY THIS CARD—Use it on Election Day. It will guide you to your polling place.

For this election, where permitted by law, two or more precincts have been consolidated, and for that reason you may find the above designated polling place away from the location where you usually vote.

Polls will be open from 6 a.m. to 7 p.m.

G. E. WADE, County Clerk.

CHAS. R. MULGREW, *Printer*

Like today, voters receive notices about where their voting location is. This notice from 1935 shows the Riverside Hotel as the local voting place. Also like today, Tuesday was the day for elections.

George Oaks started the *Alvarado Pioneer*, a newspaper covering the Alvarado area, in 1929. The newspaper was run from and printed in this small building. The building sat along the road to Mount Eden (now Union City Boulevard), just north of Smith Street.

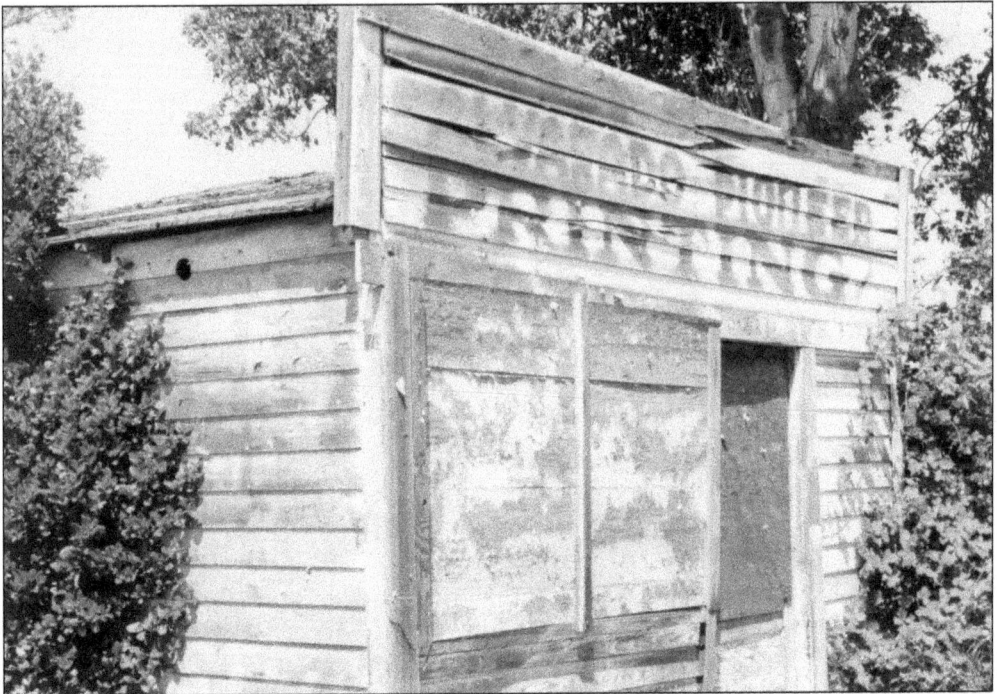

The Alvarado Pioneer Printing Building was demolished with the widening of Union City Boulevard in 1976. The *Alvarado Pioneer* would cease publishing in the 1950s.

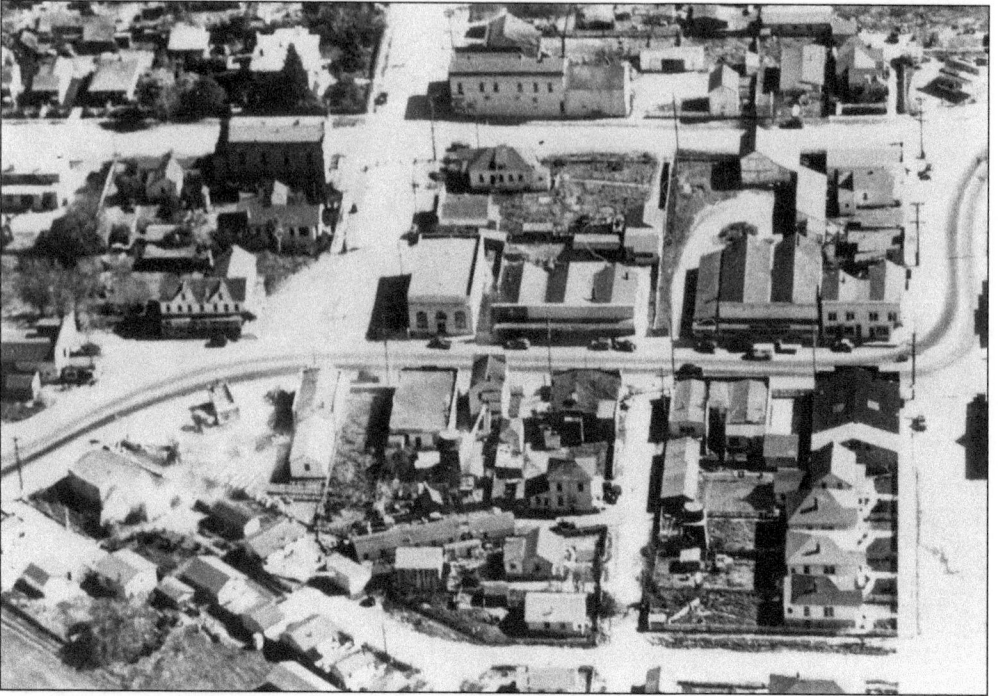

This aerial photograph of Alvarado, taken around the 1930s, shows the way Union City Boulevard looked before the road widening in 1976. The photograph is looking east. The buildings on the west side of Union City Boulevard were demolished, and the southbound lanes of Union City Boulevard were put through. The dark pattern on the road shows the route of Highway 17, which came from Hayward, turned left onto Horner Street, and continued to Centerville (Fremont) as does present-day Alvarado Boulevard, which becomes Fremont Boulevard in Fremont.

This aerial photograph from 1936 clearly shows that despite it being a town, the farm is not too far from Alvarado. Within a few blocks from the heart of Alvarado are a number of farm fields. The top part of the picture shows the sugar factory with the line of trees marking the flow of Alameda Creek. The second St. Anne's Church, built in 1926, can easily be seen just about the middle of the photograph.

This is what Union City Boulevard looked like before it was widened in 1976. On the left is the Copacabana, originally the Central Bank Building. On the right, the brick building is the Alvarado meat market. Just past it is the old Alvarado Theater.

George Althouse owned the Henry Smith house at the end of Vallejo Street, pictured here. (Courtesy Alice Robie.)

Built in about 1890, this was the Harvey Store, and for many years it was the Dinsmore store. Most recently, it has been a pizza parlor, first as Uncle Joe's Pizza and now as Bronco Billy's Pizza. It is rumored to have a ghost named Sam.

This picture shows a more recent view of the old Dinsmore store, now Bronco Billy's Pizza, from the store's parking lot.

Phillip Hellwig purchased a meat company from his cousin in 1864 and renamed it the Hellwig Meat Company. The business would expand and have retail stores in Alvarado, Hayward, and Pleasanton. When Phillip passed away in 1901, his son George took over the company. The business was well established for many years in Alvarado. This relatively recent photograph shows the slaughterhouse building used by Hellwig Meat Company. The buildings were demolished to make way for the Union City Gymnasium.

Although this view down Union City Boulevard toward Smith Street looks almost like it does today, the road was widened after this photograph. The street runs closer to the Alvarado Hotel, now called the Smith Building, on the far left. The building on the far right, originally used by Frank George, was only recently demolished for the Alvarado Square development.

Taken in the early 1950s, this photograph is of the Alvarado Fire Department with the original Alvarado fire truck. From left to right are (sitting on the fire truck) Joe Avila, Joe Goularte, and Clarence Flores; (standing) Peter Pinto, Wilbert Hendricks, Manual Perry, Joe Dutra, Manual Silva, Al Rose, Charlie Baird, Tony Vargas, and Billy Machado; (crouched down) Joe Rose, Manual Goularte, Tony Alexander, and two unidentified men.

Katsusaburo and Fusa Matsumoto built a grocery store in 1917 on Smith Street; the store still stands today as a local convenience market. This photograph shows the Japanese Hall that was built next to the market. The Japanese Association office and pool hall were downstairs, and the second story was used for boarding. The building burned down in 1924.

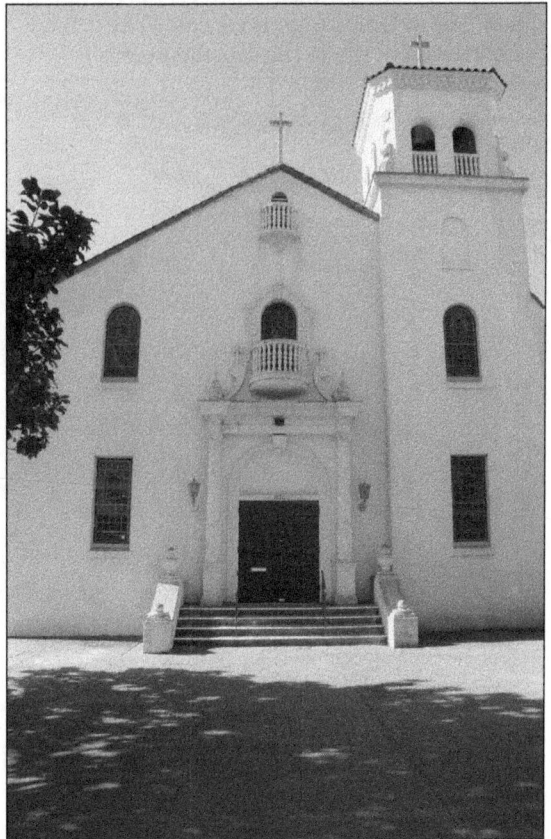

Built in 1926 in the mission revival style, the second St. Anne's Church sits on the same lot as the original church. The building became an ethnic mission church when the third St. Anne's Church was built in 1983.

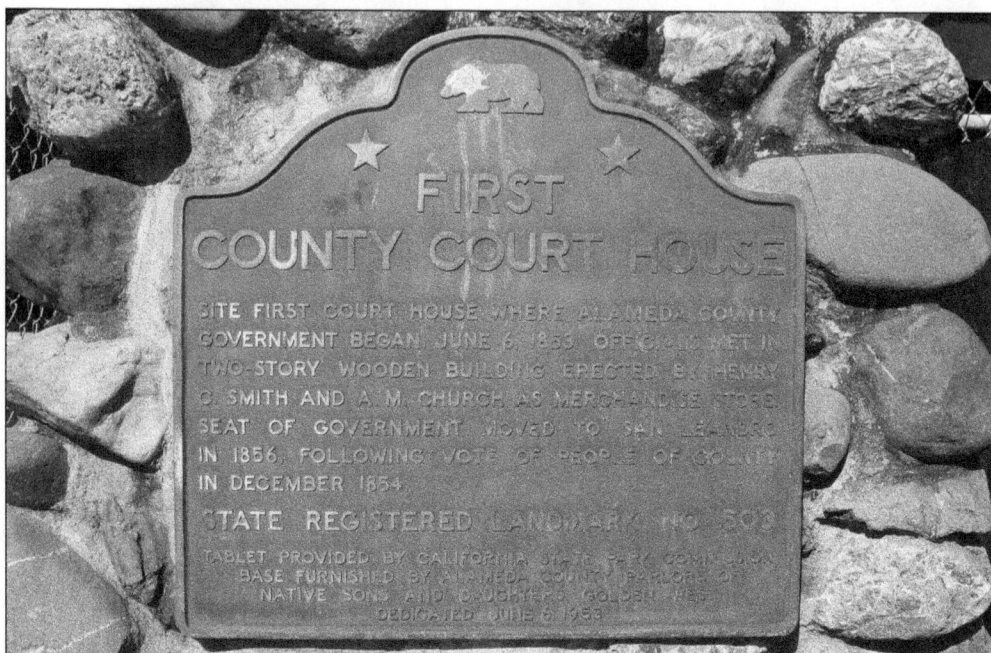

California State Historical Marker No. 503 marks the approximate location of the first Alameda County Courthouse. Since Union City Boulevard was widened, the real location of the courthouse is now part of Union City Boulevard. The marker, originally placed on June 6, 1953, sits just to the northwest of where the courthouse was.

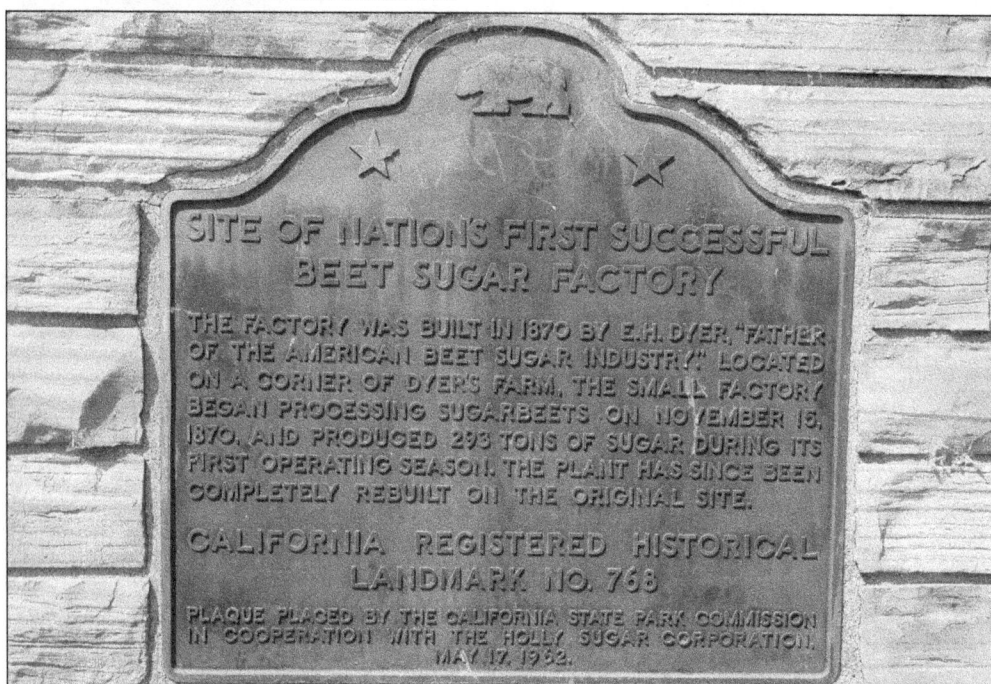

Sitting at the corner of Ratekin Street and Dyer Road, California State Historical Marker No. 768 honors the first successful sugar beet factory in the United States. This marker was place on March 17, 1962, and was moved to its present location when the factory property was redeveloped.

Two

DECOTO

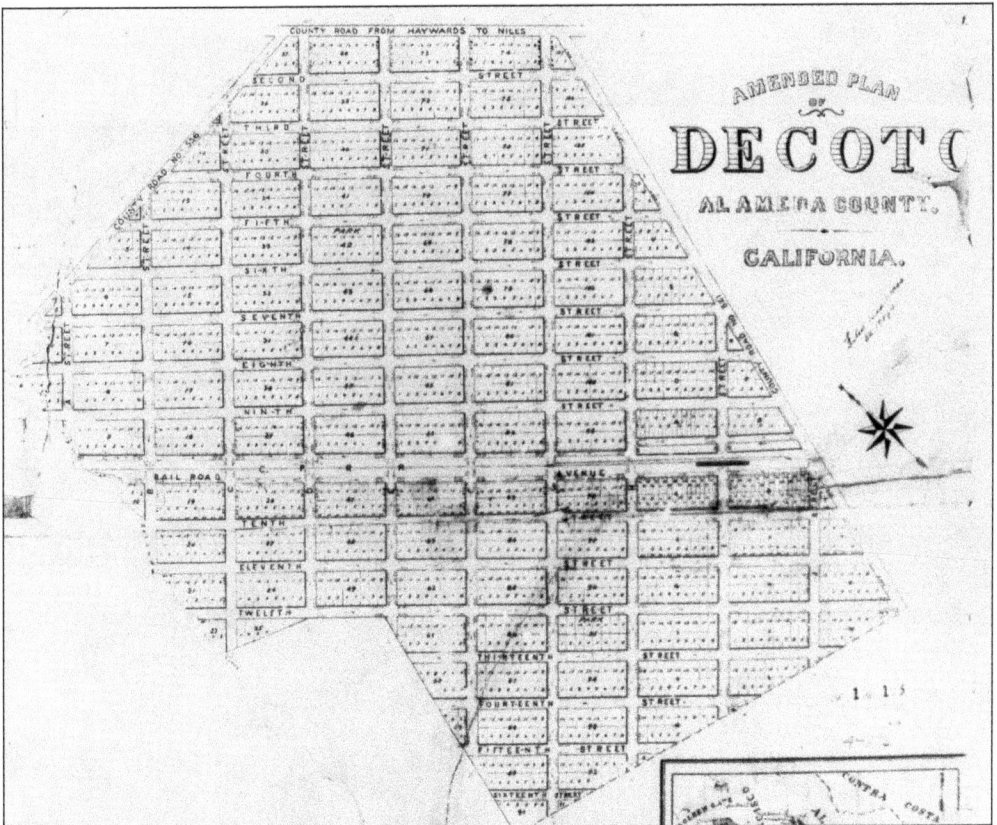

This drawing from 1878 shows the forecasted layout for Decoto with home plots and the county roads that form its borders.

Ezra Decoto, originally spelled "de Coteau," came to California in 1850 from Canada and settled in Alameda County. He and his two brothers, John and Adolphus, purchased 334 acres of land from Jonas Clark next to Mission Boulevard. The land was also adjacent to the new rail line coming through the area. (Courtesy New Haven School District.)

Jennie Lowrie, originally from Scotland, married Ezra Decoto and had a number of children. Ezra Jr. became a lawyer, district attorney, and superior court judge. Jennie and Ezra's daughter Janet married August May, the butcher. (Courtesy New Haven School District.)

In the early 1880s, the land at the end of May Road was used as picnic grounds. Many different organizations, such as the Ancient Order of United Workmen, would hold annual gatherings. This photograph shows a typical family picnic in the shade of the trees along Dry Creek. (Courtesy East Bay Regional Park District.)

The Dry Creek Picnic Grounds was the place in the Alvarado and Decoto area to hold a picnic. Many local organizations, such as the Ancient Order of United Workmen, would hold annual picnics. The biggest picnic held at the grounds every year was on the Fourth of July. Different events, from shooting contests to anvil shoots, were popular. The picnic grounds, just outside Dry Creek Cottage at the end of May Road, were close enough to the Decoto train stations that carriages would ferry picnic goers to the picnics.

Around 1900, the May family built a summer cottage and gardens next to Dry Creek close to where the old picnic grounds were. The land passed to the Meyers family when Bertha May married Henry Meyers. This photograph shows the Meyers Dry Creek Cottage decorated for the Fourth of July. (Courtesy East Bay Regional Park District.)

Standing in front of the May house is Clara May and her daughters Gertrude and Marjorie in 1897. The home still stands at the end of May Road. Clara's husband, Henry May, is the son of August May. Clara is the daughter of Charles Whipple (brother to J. C. Whipple) and Charlotte Hawley. The May house was created out of the Cosmopolitan schoolhouse and moved to the end of May Road around 1883.

In July 1868, the Cosmopolitan School District was formed near Decoto. Local pioneers like Henry Smith, Ezra Decoto, and F. Meyer served on the district board. Jonas Clark donated land just off Mission Boulevard for the schoolhouse. The Cosmopolitan School District would be divided into the Valle Vista, Decoto, and Tennyson School Districts. The schoolhouse was moved and became the May house at the end of May Road.

Crossing Alameda Creek on what is now Decoto Road is the Bell Ranch Bridge. The bridge was located near the Bell Ranch, owned by James Hawley, which was named for having one of the original mission bells hung from a tree. It was said that boats could navigate as far up Alameda Creek as the Bell Ranch Bridge.

Railroad Avenue runs along the eastern railroad tracks through Decoto. This photograph shows the bridge on Railroad Avenue crossing Dry Creek as it meanders toward Alameda Creek.

Whipple Road is named after the Whipple family, who owned a large farm along the road. The main house for the farm was built in 1852 by J. C. Whipple from "shiplap" boards. As the family grew, it was expanded. The front of the house was added on in the 1870s. This particular picture is from the 1953 picnic of the Washington Township Historical Society, which still exists today. The Whipple farm would eventually become an industrial part of Union City.

Another view of the J. C. Whipple house shows the back of the house, which was the original structure.

Brother to John C. Whipple, Edwin Whipple came to the area around 1878 with his wife, Emily. Edwin was active in the Masons and was a trustee of the Masonic home. Edwin also served on the Decoto School Board. This photograph shows their house on the Whipple property.

The Decoto Public School was built the 1880s on H Street. The Decoto School District was formed from part of the Cosmopolitan School District. This schoolhouse would be used until 1925, when a new school was built.

In 1898, the Masons built the Home for Orphans and Widows on a hill in Decoto. This photograph shows the opening ceremonies. Eventually the orphans would be moved to Covina, California, in 1926 and the widow's home would be opened to all retired Masons. The main building would have two wings added, and other buildings would create a Masonic campus. The main building still exists and was recently gutted and renovated to last another 100 years.

A front view of the Masonic Home for Orphans and Widows looks from Mission Boulevard. Where the orchards are growing below the home became a well-known gladiola field.

In 1910, the Alameda County supervisor and the Oakland Free Library signed a pact to create county libraries in the unincorporated towns. This undated photograph shows the Decoto Library. The sign says the library was open Saturday and Sunday from 2:00 to 5:00 p.m. and 7:00 to 8:00 p.m. on Monday, Wednesday, and Friday.

This image shows Anthony Dutra dressed in his army uniform in Decoto. He was known for playing on local baseball teams like the Alvarado Eagles and a team formed by Kraft Tile in Niles. The photograph was taken between 1941 and 1945. (Courtesy Carol Dutra-Vernaci.)

Standing at the corner of Fourth and F Streets is the Dutra family just before World War II. Second from the left is Marie Dutra Lee, with Elsie Dutra third from the left. Behind Elsie is her husband, Henry Dutra, and on the right end is Frank Dutra. Note that the streets were still dirt. The larger home on the right still exists, but the smaller homes in the background are no longer there. (Courtesy Carol Dutra-Vernaci.)

This aerial photograph from 1941 shows the core part of Decoto bordered by Whipple and Decoto Roads. At the top of the photograph, covered by trees, is Dry Creek Cottage, and beyond that is what is now Dry Creek/Pioneer Regional Park. In the middle of the photograph, close to the railroad tracks, are a number of canneries.

This aerial photograph from 1950 shows Decoto and the area around it. On the left side of the picture is Dry Creek, coming from the hills and meandering toward the bay. On the right is Decoto Road. At the lower part of the photograph is Alvarado-Niles Road. In the distance is Mount Diablo.

At 4:28 a.m. on the morning of August 24, 1951, United Airlines Flight 615 crashed in Tolman Peak just east of Decoto. The four-engine DC-6 hit the knoll on Tolman Peak, flipped over, and crashed on the other side. Fuel explosions caused parts of the plane to roll down a ravine. All 50 persons on the flight were killed. In this photograph, the small clump of trees in the center is the knoll on Tolman Peak.

This photograph shows a First Communion class at the original Our Lady of the Rosary Church, built in 1907. (Courtesy Our Lady of the Rosary.)

The Decoto School District existed until the New Haven Unified School District was created. This 1956 photograph shows the board from the Decoto School District. From left to right are (seated) Joseph Sloan Jr., Manual White, and Charles Plummer; (standing) H. Alvin Searles.

Gil Prevette from Decoto raced stock cars at the San Jose Speedway. Gil would drive the Union City Special 66X and Union City Special II cars over a number of years. In October 1960, he won first place after being cheered on by 80 Union City Little League players. The week after that was Gil Prevette Night, honoring him and celebrating his 24th birthday. (Courtesy Gil Prevette.)

The Union City Merchants and Businessmen's Association sponsored Union City Night at the San Jose Speedway, where both Gil Prevette and Al Cease were racing. Councilman Tom Kitayama attended to hand out the winning trophy to Gil Prevette. From left to right are Kitayama, Gil Prevette, Union City Queen Pat Whittler, Joseph Calderia, Marshall Sargent, and Susan Guptill. (Courtesy Gil Prevette.)

The Union City
Merchants and
Businessmen's Association
sponsored this event in
both 1961 and 1962. The
tickets were printed by
Kelly's Garage, which
sponsored Gil Prevette,
and Williams Brothers
Construction. (Courtesy
Gil Prevette.)

UNION CITY NIGHT

SATURDAY — JUNE 23, 1962

SAN JOSE
SPEEDWAY

8 P. M.

Sponsored by the Union City Merchants

| THIS TICKET THROUGH COURTESY OF YOUR **WILLIAMS BROS.** CONSTR. CO., INC. EXCAVATING, GRADING, PAVING **KELLY'S GARAGE** | Exchange This Ticket At The Box Office For A REGULAR $175 TICKET | PAY ONLY $1.00 |

Two of the Union City racers were Al and John Cease, who drove the Union City Extra Special car. Prevette and the Cease brothers would duke it out every Saturday night at the raceway. When Prevette had some back luck with transmission problems, John Cease was able to win a few races. Al Cease would roll the car one night, spend the week fixing the damage, and return the next week to have a winning performance. (Courtesy Gil Prevette.)

Started in 1937, Pacific States Steel would be a fixture of Decoto for 40 years. This early photograph of Pacific States Steel shows the factory buildings and the pond. (Courtesy Karl Vincent.)

This shows the factory from the south with the railroad tracks just to the west of the factory. At the lower right is the crossing of Alvarado-Niles Road and the railroad tracks. This is the present border of Union City and Fremont (then Decoto and Niles, respectively), which gave the factory a Niles address.

A later photograph of Pacific States Steel shows the expanded factory. With early American cars being built primarily of steel, car bodies were recycled, melted, and reused to make new steel. The junked cars were brought in on rail cars and stored at the factory.

Cars brought to the factory on rail cars were moved from the storage pile by being picked up by a crane and placed on a conveyor and then into the factory to be melted down. (Courtesy Karl Vincent.)

This inside view of the Pacific State Steel factory shows the large crucible used for pouring steel. (Courtesy Karl Vincent.)

Three

UNION CITY

At the very first Union City Council meeting, held on January 26, 1959, the city council was sworn in and Union City was officially a city. The first action of the city council was to appoint Tom Kitayama as the first mayor, making him the first Japanese American mayor in the United States. Tom was appointed mayor because he had the highest number of votes from the city council election. (Courtesy Heidi Kitayama.)

In late 1959, after months of fund-raising, the ground-breaking ceremony was held for the new church building at Our Lady of the Rosary Church in Decoto. From left to right, holding the shovel, are Mayor Tom Kitayama, Fr. Tom Rielly, and Harold Schoenfeld, superintendent of the Decoto School District. (Courtesy Our Lady of the Rosary Church.)

Part of the job of a mayor is to be a spokesperson for the city. Here Mayor Tom Kitayama sits for a press photograph for the March of Dimes.

Council members John Ratekin (left) and Tom Kitayama (second from the left) pose with the Newark and Union City City Council Championship bowling trophy. The championship was sponsored by Seagram's and held at Lido Lanes in Newark.

After incorporation, the Alvarado Fire Station on Smith Street became Union City Fire Station No. 2. The original Alvarado fire truck, on the left, was donated to the Alameda County Fair and sat at the fairgrounds for many years. The city was able to get the fire truck back, and it resides in its original home at the Alvarado Fire Station, now the Union City Historical Museum.

Once Union City incorporated, the Decoto Fire Station on Tenth Street was turned into Union City Fire Station No. 1. The original Decoto 1938 Van Pelt fire truck, the second truck from the left, is still owned by Union City and is used for special events.

Standing next to an early map of Union City are Alameda County supervisor John Murphy (left) and John Ratekin. The map is the General Plan extending out to 1980.

Sitting in the mayor's office in 1963 is Mayor John Ratekin (left) with Alameda County supervisor John Murphy.

At the corner of Horner Street and Union City Boulevard was Priego's Market, part of the Red and White chain of markets. Third from the left is Dane Priego.

To expand its church, Hillview Baptist Church purchased an old barracks building from the Alameda Naval Air Station and had it moved to Union City in 1959. The building was used for Sunday school and Vacation Bible School classrooms. (Courtesy Hillview Baptist Church.)

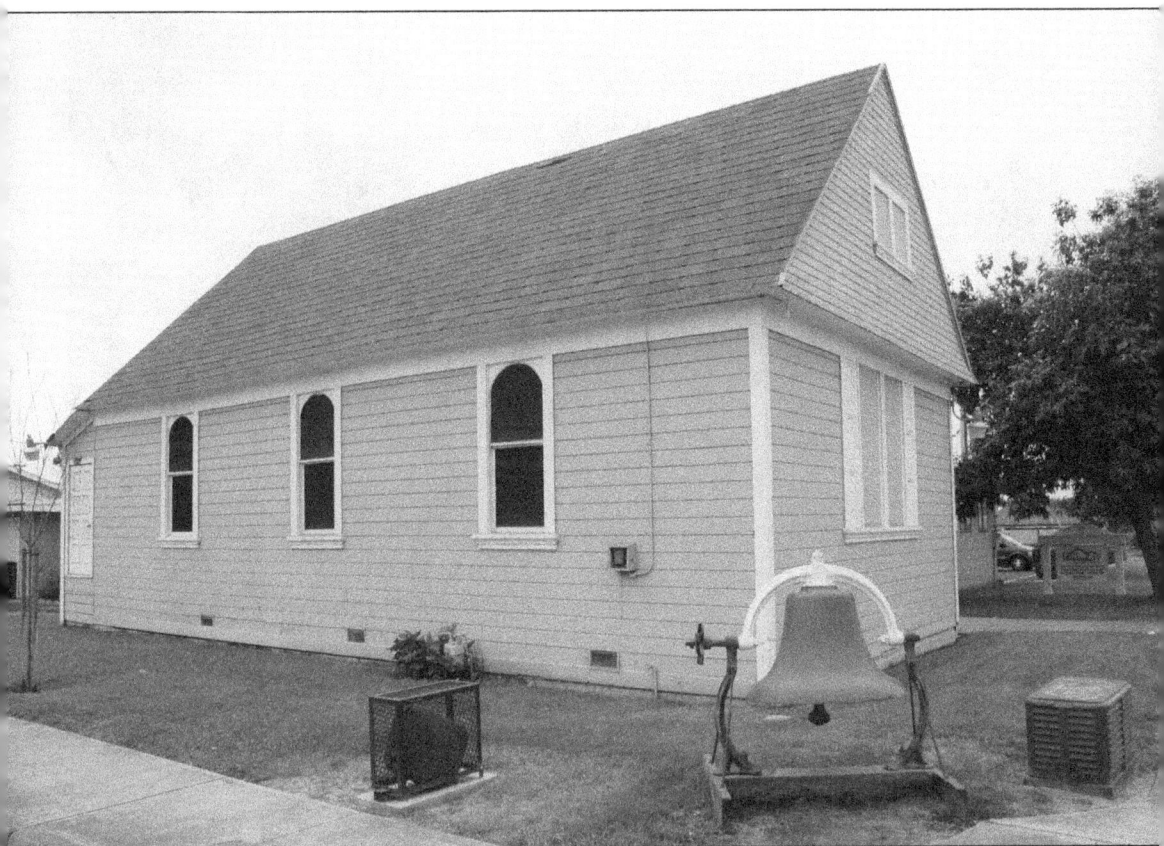

On January 11, 1978, a fire broke out at Hillview Baptist Church, destroying the bell tower. Union City firefighters were able to remove the original bell from the tower. The bell, cast in 1873, was repaired by Ron Musgrove and placed on display next to the church at the corner of H and Ninth Streets.

The Meyers daughters, Edith, Mildred, and Jeanette, would spend their summers at Dry Creek Cottage and use it to host fund-raising events. This photograph from the late 1960s shows a gathering at Dry Creek Cottage. In the background is the cabana next to the swimming pool. (Courtesy East Bay Regional Park District.)

In 1967, Our Lady of the Rosary Church created an elementary school. The school building was moved from the Decoto Elementary School where it was going to be demolished to make way for a new school. (Courtesy Our Lady of the Rosary Church.)

In 1966, the Union City Police Department was formed. Previously the police duties were done by the Alameda County Sheriff on contract to Union City. City hall, at Whipple Road and Central Avenue, had to be expanded to accommodate the new department. This photograph shows the back of that expansion and a number of police cars. (Courtesy of City of Union City.)

Built in 1966, the Union City Drive-In would serve the Union City area for 32 years, closing in March 1998 to make way for the Union Landing Shopping Center and the Century 25 Theaters. It was the last active drive-in theater in Alameda County.

On October 12, 1974, Union City started bus service with "The Flea." The Union City Transit bus system augmented the A/C Transit public transit system with routes that covered more parts of Union City. (Courtesy Carol Dutra-Vernaci.)

On June 11, 1974, Union City police chief William Cann was assassinated. While he attended a community meeting at Our Lady of the Rosary Church, shots were fired through a window in the church hall, striking Chief Cann in the neck and striking three other people. On August 29, Chief Cann died from his wounds, having never regained consciousness. This photograph shows the side of the hall from where the shots came.

After police chief William Cann was assassinated, Union City dedicated a park to him as the William Cann Memorial Park. On September 7, 1975, a memorial grove was planted in honor of Chief Cann. His wife, Elizabeth, and his son Chris assisted with the planting.

Little League has been popular in Union City for a long time. This photograph shows the Teamsters baseball team from the Union City Little League of 1969.

From Our Lady of the Rosary School, the Tiger cheerleaders and a little "mascot" are pictured. (Courtesy of Our Lady of the Rosary Church.)

Pictured here is the fourth-grade basketball team from the Our Lady of the Rosary School, then named the Holy Rosary School. (Courtesy of Our Lady of the Rosary Church.)

The eighth-grade basketball team from the Our Lady of the Rosary School is shown. Standing on the far right is Pat Mullen. (Courtesy of Our Lady of the Rosary Church.)

This view down Smith Street shows a couple of storefronts with Manny's Dancing on the left. Seen above the buildings is the second St. Anne's Church. All three buildings exist today.

Girl Scout cookies are a popular and well-known fund-raiser for Girl Scout troops. Here girls from Union City Troop 1686 discuss the cookies with a local teacher in the early 1970s. (Courtesy Anne Riojas.)

Despite being a city for 11 years, Union City did not have a flag until Anne Riojas and local Girl Scouts remedied this situation by handcrafting this flag based on the city seal. On July 20, 1970, Girl Scout Renee Louie presents the flag to the city council. (Courtesy Anne Riojas.)

Carrying the flag they created, local Girl Scouts parade down H Street as part of the Fiesta Days parade in a picture from August 8, 1970. (Courtesy Anne Riojas.)

This photograph from the late 1970s, taken for a local newspaper, shows Union City police officer Jim Povidenza sitting in his patrol car.

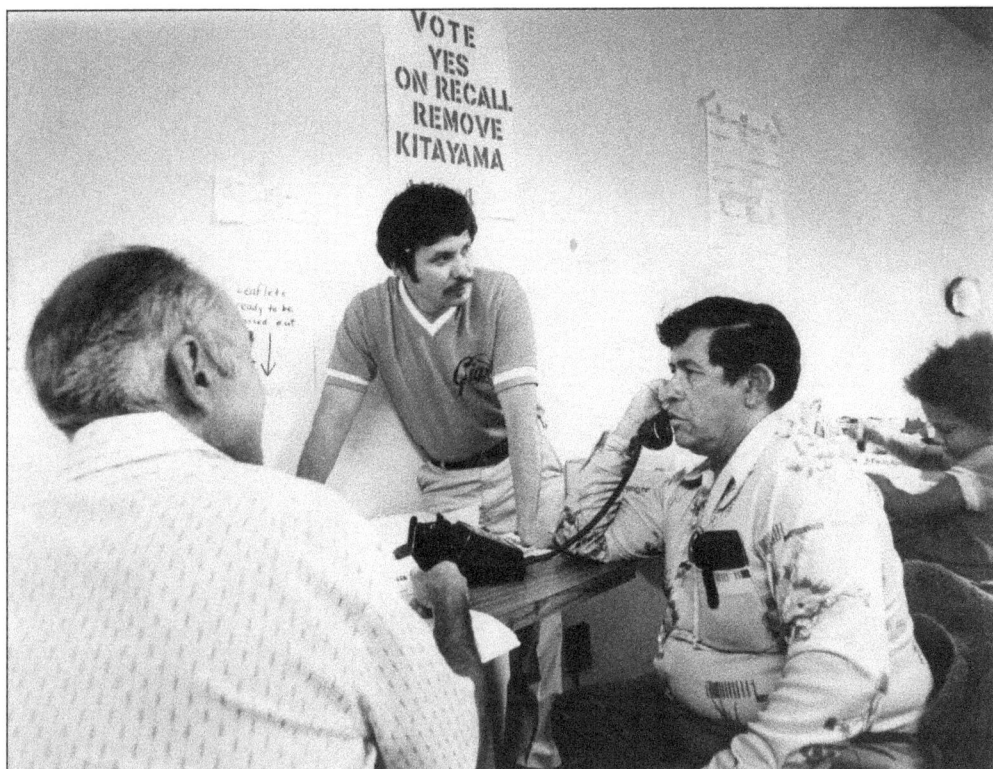

During his career as a publicly elected mayor, Tom Kitayama faced one recall election. It was partially organized by a labor union trying to unionize the laborers working for Kitayama's flower business. Helping with the recall campaign was César Chávez (on the phone).

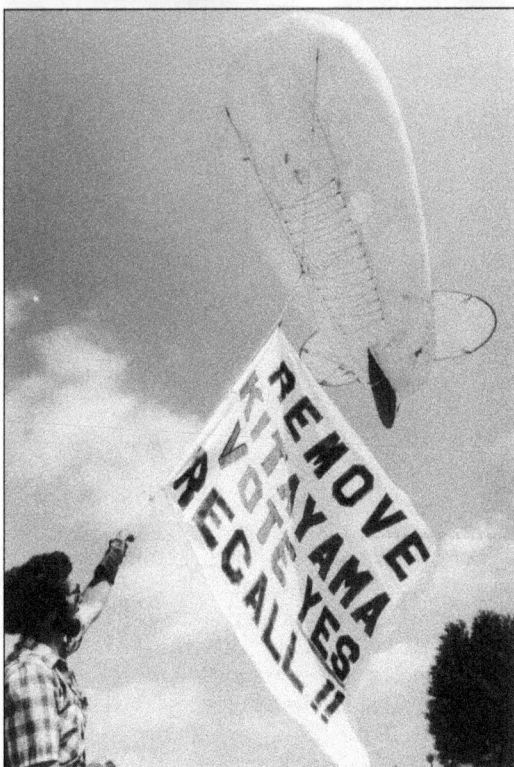

This balloon was used to advertise the recall election of Mayor Tom Kitayama.

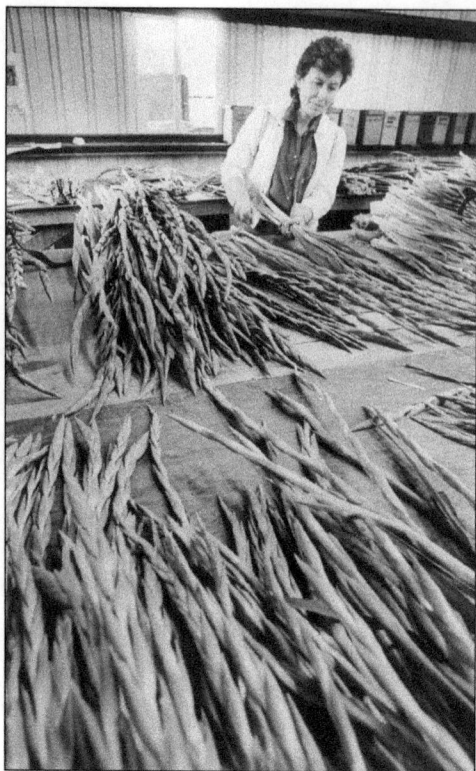

Gladiolas were a popular crop in Union City, so much so that in 1985 the Gladiola Festival was created in Union City. The gladiola was also used in the first city seal.

Part of growing gladiolas was the preparation of the fields. Methyl bromide was used to fumigate the fields before planting. In the background is the Pacific State Steel factory. This places the field just to the east of the factory and to the west of Mission Boulevard. Gladiolas were also grown in the fields just in front and north of the Masonic home.

120

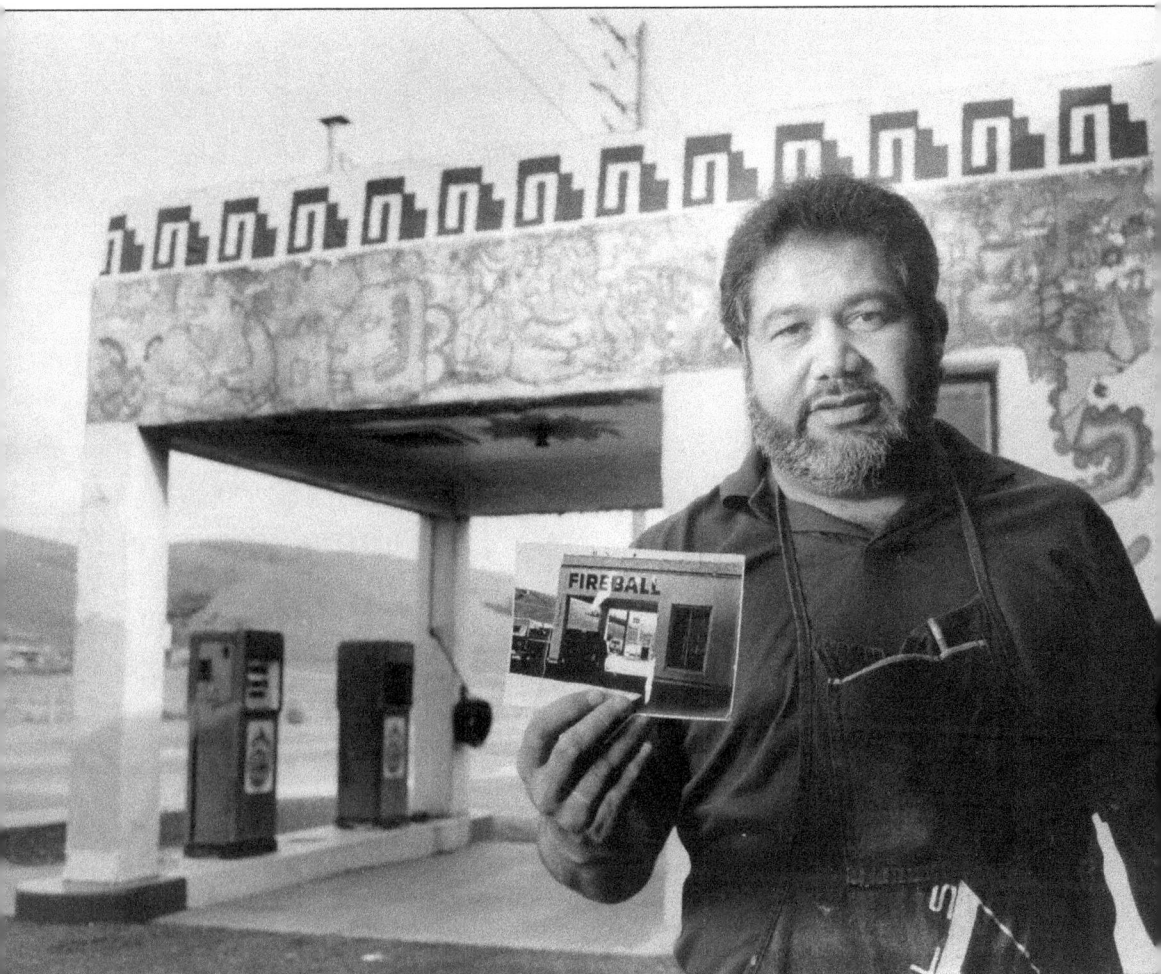

The Teen Workshop on Mission Boulevard was originally the Fireball gas station. Holding a picture of the original gas station is Larry Orozco, who ran the Teen Workshop at the time this picture of him was taken. Larry Orozco currently runs the Ruggieri Senior Center.

Started in 1974 by Richard Valle, Jaime Jaramillo, and Frank Roesch, Centro de Servicios is a provider of services to low-income and immigrant families. The thrift store is housed in a Quonset hut that was originally owned and operated by the Rodriguez family.

In November 1996, the 50th anniversary of the World War II Veterans Memorial was celebrated. Originally the memorial was located in Decoto, but it was later moved to Kennedy Park. The veterans identified in this photograph include Anthony Dutra (first row, third from the right), Decoto fireman Al Rodriguez (first row, fourth from the right), David Berrios (second row, third from right), and Dilbert Costa (fourth from the left).

Built in 1998 on land that was formerly the Kitayama Nursery, Tom Kitayama Elementary School was designed to have Asian aspects, including the blue tile roof and the design of the gables.

When Kitayama Elementary School was dedicated, Tom Kitayama, pictured here, gave the opening speech. (Courtesy Heidi Kitayama.)

Built in the same location as the Loyola House, the Loyola Building, constructed in 2000, houses a coffee shop, restaurant, and a number of small businesses. This building, plus the weekly farmer's market, has brought some life back into old Alvarado.

Celebration of Life

Tom Kitayama

July 13, 1923 – June 5, 2007

On June 5, 2007, Tom Kitayama passed away. He was the last of the original members of the Union City City Council. On June 16, a service was held to celebrate the life of Tom Kitayama. Many city, local, and county officials attended the service to honor the former mayor. This collage of photographs was created by the Kitayama family to be used on the cover of the program for the service. (Courtesy Heidi Kitayama.)

126

BIBLIOGRAPHY

Country Club of Washington Township. *History of Washington Township*. Stanford, CA: Stanford University Press, 1962.

City of Union City. *Looking Back: Early Glimpses of Union City*. Union City, CA: self-published, 1978.

Sandoval, John. *History of Washington Township*. Hayward, CA: Mount Eden Publishers, 1985.

Thompson and West. *Official and Historical Atlas of Alameda County, California*. Fresno, CA: Valley Publishers, 1976.

Wood, M. W. *History of Alameda County, California*. Oakland, CA: self-published. 1883.

Visit us at
arcadiapublishing.com

www.ingramcontent.com/pod-product-compliance
Lightning Source LLC
Chambersburg PA
CBHW050605110426
42813CB00008B/2462